A Chair For All Seasons
Celebrating the Adirondack Chair

Written by Kathleen Graham Kelly
Photography by Karen Williamson

Copyright © 2019 Kathleen Graham Kelly.

All rights reserved. No part of this book may be used or reproduced by any means, graphic, electronic, or mechanical, including photocopying, recording, taping or by any information storage retrieval system without the written permission of the author except in the case of brief quotations embodied in critical articles and reviews.

Balboa Press books may be ordered through booksellers or by contacting:

Balboa Press
A Division of Hay House
1663 Liberty Drive
Bloomington, IN 47403
www.balboapress.com
1 (877) 407-4847

Because of the dynamic nature of the Internet, any web addresses or links contained in this book may have changed since publication and may no longer be valid. The views expressed in this work are solely those of the author and do not necessarily reflect the views of the publisher, and the publisher hereby disclaims any responsibility for them.

Copyright on all photographs in this book is held by Karen A. Williamson, the photographer. To obtain fine art prints or inquire about usage rights, go to karenwilliamsonphoto.photoshelter.com.

ISBN: 978-1-9822-1542-2 (sc)
ISBN: 978-1-9822-1541-5 (e)

Library of Congress Control Number: 2018912992

Print information available on the last page.

Balboa Press rev. date: 12/10/2018

Dedications

Kathleen's Dedication
For those who love the Adirondacks
and for Rosemary and Everett.

Karen's Dedication
For all the family, friends, and clients who have encouraged and
supported my Adirondack chair habit through the years.

Introduction

Perhaps something like this has happened to you. After I leased a red Honda CRV, I began to see the same car everywhere. I never noticed so many red Hondas before, and then I began to see red cars of every make and model. Were they always on the road and I just didn't pay attention?

This also happened to me with Adirondack chairs over the past twenty years. Adirondack chairs were always there in the background where I grew up in upstate New York. But once I started paying attention, they were everywhere: on signs, logos, calendars, posters, stationery, jewelry, dish towels, tote bags, playing cards ... everywhere! Huge Volkswagen Beetle-sized Adirondack chairs advertised a roadside truck stop. Rows of Adirondack chairs appeared in advertising for everything from campgrounds to vacation loans--even an ad for flooring installation.

What is it about Adirondack chairs, I asked myself, that so deeply speaks to people? Why is this image found in so many different contexts? I began asking people what the Adirondack chair image means to them. The answers were often paradoxical. Some people said "solitude;" others said "togetherness." Some said "silent reflection;" others said "celebration." Many mentioned "escape," "vacation," "renewal," or "carefree freedom." Almost every person mentioned some variation of relaxing in the outdoors, rest, and tuning in to the natural world. I began to think of an Adirondack chair as an icon; something that conveys a depth of meaning and insight instantly. Adirondack chairs trigger treasured memories and speak to people on an emotional level: Adirondack chairs…ahhh, peace!

This book was inspired by a collection of photographs by Karen Williamson, a photographer from upstate New York. Her work often features an Adirondack chair or groups of chairs captured in natural settings. My first vision for the book was a series of photographs of the Adirondack chair in different seasons. Then I connected the Adirondack chair to the seasons of life, which made perfect sense to me, considering my academic background in life history and adult development. The result is one fictional woman's life story, represented by the seasons of life and the seasons of the northeastern United States -- anchored throughout by her treasured Adirondack chair.

You may look at this book and wonder, "What kind of book is it? A children's book? A memoir? A photo book with text?" Consider it all of the above. The character Rosie is loosely based on the author's mother, Rosemary Ann Murphy Graham (1926-2006). The sensory details of the seasons are memories of fifty years of the author's Adirondack adventures with friends and family.

I hope you enjoy it, whatever your season in your life cycle.

Rosie In Her Late Winter

My 90th birthday party will be later today. In the morning light I look out the back window of my tiny apartment at my green Adirondack chair sitting quietly in the snow of my mini backyard, waiting for washing, sanding, and new paint. The Westport chair in particular has been part of every season of my life ... there is something special about that ...

Spring

Spring: a time of streams bulging with snowmelt surging over boulders and pebbles. Gushing waterfalls spill over rock ledges. Chunks of debris are pulled from their moorings by the rushing waters and carried downstream, where they clog the stream channel. The clogged stream overtops its banks and the floodwaters fill cellars and threaten buildings. The lake level rises, creeping up the protective concrete wall along the shore, nudging toward the 100-year flood mark for the second time in three years. The floating dock rises above its moorings, freeing the boats we thought were tied securely.

The weather is unpredictable: a cold snap turns fields into icy marshes and parking lots into skating rinks. Then the first warm spell nudges tiny crocuses from the soil through the snow. Daffodils and tulips follow. As the weather continues to warm, yellow

dandelions take over the lawn and spring peepers sing in the woods. Overnight the buds start to burst, and tiny pastel yellow and green leaves emerge.

In early spring, farmers harvest sap flowing from the veins of the maple tree and boil it down for syrup and sugar. Later, the warming earth yields asparagus, early peas and lettuce. Easter comes, and with it treats of chocolate, malted milk balls and jellybeans, colored eggs hidden around the pond, and chocolate melted in the early spring sunshine.

Rosie's Spring Memories

In the spring of my life, I remember sitting on my Grampy's lap in the Westport chair. While he drank his coffee, I watched the birds returning north and the chipmunks scampering across the crunchy leaves of early spring.

The Westport chair is considered to be the first design of what today is called the Adirondack chair. It was created in Westport, New York; hence its name. We were lucky to have one that was saved by Grace Smith, a cousin of my uncle.

The Great Depression meant my mother, sister, brothers, and I didn't have much of anything; Dad disappeared when the financial tough times came. He did rejoin the family from afar and through our growing years we saw him every other Saturday afternoon. We moved into Grandma's rental flat in the city and left most of our furniture behind in our rural home. But we did take that Westport chair; we put it in the shared, tiny backyard at Grandma's house. The chair was an island of serenity and escape from a crowded house. Ah … that chair was a ticket to another place.

As teenagers during World War II, there weren't many places for us to go. I went to high school by day and then worked a 3-11 p.m. shift as a clerk at a state office near the New York State Capitol to help support my family.

It didn't seem difficult then, and I didn't know we were poor. This was just what my sister and I did. We left our high school classes and took the bus downtown. I had to alter my date of birth on my Social Security card to begin employment. Our mother sold bread on the street. On the weekends my sister and I sat in our Westport chair in the tiny backyard, read letters from our brothers and other GIs, and thought about Frank Sinatra. Oh yes ... my high school friends and I snuck our first cigarettes and illegal drinks in that chair too!

Summer

Summer: A too-short season of long, hot days interrupted by quick, violent thunderstorms. A lazy mountain river, still full of spring's bounty of water, gently carries canoes and kayaks toward the lake.

The lake is the center of summer life. Turtles sun themselves on the rocks, while a dozen baby ducklings parade behind their mama down the shoreline, slipping under the docks and popping up like bobbers. Fishermen and women, young and old, spend long, lazy days angling from the dock, passing the time alone in the sunshine as gentle waves lap the shoreline. Look! A catch … but wait; a bigger fish took possession before the medium-sized catch could be reeled in. The youngest are thrilled to catch any fish, of any size.

Boats are everywhere. Water skiers seek the calm, glassy water of early morning and dusk; while first-time skiers get up, only to tumble into the huge watery gully made by the boat's wake. Kids scream as they are towed on tubes pulled by powerboats driven by uncles. Sailboats tack across the bay on a breeze, but are left adrift when the breeze unexpectedly dies.

Summer is family vacation time at the lake. Kids skip stones across the calm water. Day hikers hold a contest to see who can collect the most salamanders. Kids row across the lake to pitch a tent for an overnight adventure on the island, or swim to the island with a friend in the rowboat alongside. A family goes camping on a mountain, but their tent is blown down the mountainside with the kids inside! All survive with a funny story to tell. And if it rains, there is the luxury of reading an entire book nonstop in a rustic cabin.

Summer food is the best. Hot dogs definitely taste better stuck on sticks and cooked over a wood fire. Unable to wait for their s'mores, kids burn their marshmallows – but really don't care. Everyone savors the aromas of breakfast at camp: bacon, eggs, and potatoes cooked on the Coleman stove. And then there are jewels of the harvest: gorgeous, red-ripe, home-grown tomatoes; plump peppers; eggplant; and broccoli. The berries of summer are picked and made into delicious pies, cakes, and cobblers; as well as precious jams and preserves.

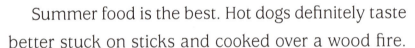

Rosie's Summer Memories

Summer was the prime of my life. I grew and prospered, pursuing opportunities and conquering challenges. I thought that summer would go on forever.

In the 1950s and 60s I found love, married at 23, and started my own family. I was the first in the family to purchase my own home; it was a big accomplishment to not be renters. The home was a two-family in the city, like my grandmother's house. We had a small front and back yard, a detached garage, and tenants upstairs. The rental income from the tenants made home-ownership possible for us. My husband and I welcomed four children in ten years. Our possessions grew, including a blue Chevy when my dad died. This was a big improvement, giving us freedom from the city bus schedule and making grocery shopping and visiting relatives much easier.

One of those new-to-us possessions was the old Westport chair. We put it in our own small backyard. As the years went by, we added another chair: an official wooden Adirondack chair from Sears. Our children grew up using the two Adirondack chairs in the shared backyard for escape, serenity, dreaming, crying, stargazing, screaming in fury, sunbathing, listening to a new transistor radio, and seeking solitude – just as I had used the Westport chair at my grandmother's house.

As children do, ours grew up and went their separate and independent ways. Then, my husband died. I was alone again.

Our eldest child bought her first house on a small lake. It made sense to give her the Westport and Adirondack chairs as a housewarming gift. The lake was the perfect place for those chairs, set on the shore for watching the birds by day and the stars by night.

My mom passed on in the late 1970's. We gathered sadly at the lake to pay tribute to her. We shared memories, looked at old pictures and

slides, and watched family movies. We sat in the Adirondack chairs and remembered, together.

My first grandchild learned to stand by holding on to the Westport chair. He and I cuddled and huddled in the chair, wrapped in blankets. We read story books, watched sunsets, and came to love each other in that special way of grandparents and grandchildren.

My second grandchild brought more joy and love, as she put her doll babies to sleep in the Westport chair, and insisted on eating her macaroni and cheese only in that chair.

Time went on, and more grandkids joined the clutch. Eventually there were eight grandbabies and each brought his or her unique energy and gifts. One eleven-month period brought three new babies! The times when we were all together were rare and precious, sometimes tense, and sometimes sad; but I always treasured them. I mourned that loss of togetherness when we went our separate ways at summer's end.

Summer at the lake was always filled with memory-making moments. One year the grandkids used the Adirondack chairs to dry their towels after swimming, and then built a fort with the chairs as the framework. They decided to sleep outside overnight in the chair-and-towel fort, and added blankets for more coverage. The adventure was short-lived though; they made it to 9 p.m. before getting spooked by the outside noises and rushing into the cabin.

Another summer one grandson hosted his tenth birthday party with a dozen ten-year-old boys. There were so many drenched towels that we had to take a trip to the laundromat in a nearby town.

On muggy summer nights we sat at the edge of the lake on blankets as dusk enveloped us, counting the bats and then spotting the constellations. Bugs drove us inside to find citronella candles and insect repellent. Then we returned outside to watch for shooting stars and doze on the blankets, listening to the lapping waves.

For two summers we were fortunate to have a resident great blue heron visit very early each morning. And every year a pair or threesome of common loons completed our lakeside family. They would wake us up with their eerie call, bringing everyone out in pajamas, with binoculars ready. Sometimes they thrilled us by coming up close when the lake was quiet and still. Once my daughter was swimming quietly at dawn and surprised a drifting loon only an arm's length away.

Fall

Fall is a season painted in leaves of red, yellow, orange, and brown. The broad streams of summer shrink into trickles easily traversed by hikers. Some stream beds dry up entirely, making a handy route for hiking up mountains. Dry leaves crunch underfoot along the lakeshore. As fall progresses, nature turns slowly toward the cold dryness of the coming winter. The colors go from vibrant to dull as nature quiets everything.

Fall is a time to drink lots of hot apple cider and wish for the longer days of summer. Kids press beautiful leaves in wax paper and trace their hands to make turkey pictures. Hunting is a pastime for many; some track the white-tailed deer and others scour the woods for special pinecones for Christmas crafts. Everyone prepares for the coming winter. People stock up on wood for the stove, while chipmunks scurry about storing nuts for the long winter ahead.

And at Thanksgiving people gather to give thanks and celebrate being together.

Rosie's Fall Memories

The fall of my life was a time for reflection, a gradual slowing of the busyness of summer. I sought a new rhythm that was quieter and more peaceful, with less activity and more time to pause.

As preteens, those grandkids ran to the Adirondack chairs with their friends as soon as we arrived at the lake, sitting three to a chair, escaping the adults in their lives. As teenagers they cried and laughed while lounging across the chairs, their changing bodies leaning awkwardly over those broad chair arms. They probably snuck the same smokes and drinks that I did at their age, but of course they never told me.

One fall the hikers of the family climbed one of the toughest "46" peaks. There are 46 peaks over 4,000 feet in the Adirondack Mountains. Those who climb all 46 earn the title "Adirondack 46er." When they returned, they sat in the Adirondack chairs to loosen their hiking boots and shed layers of clothes. Their journey was a challenge met.

Through the fall of my life, I watched my own children and grandchildren age and grow. I wondered about the meaning of it all.

Winter

Winter: the first freeze of a sliver of ice on a pond, enough to hold a bird but not a stone. The waters of the lake freeze, imprisoned in place. The creek too is frozen, energy locked under the ice; sometimes emerging through a hole and then diving below the ice again.

Winter is silence, snow glittering in the light of a full moon -- an unbroken expanse save for the tracks of rabbits and deer.

Winter is icicles hanging from the edge of the roof, standing like inverted swords, weapons ready to be broken off by the young ones. Kids make snow angels, eat freshly fallen snow, and are warned not to eat yellow snow. Snow is for snowball fights, making Eskimo forts, sledding, cross-country and downhill skiing, and snowshoeing.

In winter, we ice skate and ice fish on the frozen lake. We ski out onto the lake by moonlight and listen to the groaning sounds of ice flexing beneath us. Through it all, we always return to the warmth of the fire circle and the Adirondack chairs. We gather the chairs close to the fire to capture heat and keep out the wind. Around that fire, we drink hot chocolate, glugwein, and tea made with melted snow.

Winter also brings the joy of Christmas and the promise of the new year. Some of those New Year's parties were intimate and some raucous; we welcomed one year in with the clanging of pots and pans that echoed out into the lake-side darkness.

Rosie's Winter Memories

It is now my own late winter. I pause, see the messy, melting snow outside and reflect on these memories. They are sweet memories, and fill me with joy and gratitude; but there is also sadness as I realize that my time on Earth, on this land, in these chairs, is coming close to the end. That green Westport chair has been part of my life since I was a little girl. It may be my legacy. I hope my children, my grandchildren, and my great-grandchildren will treasure the gatherings in and the solace found in my Adirondack chairs. When the next generations of kids and grandkids sit in my chairs, I hope they remember me.

Those Adirondack chairs are and have been the center of the gatherings of our lives. Family picnics, Fourth of July fireworks and bonfires, graduations, bridal showers, bachelor parties, birthdays, anniversaries, guys' ski weekends, the completion of 46er mountain challenges, dinner club gatherings, book club retreats, bon voyage parties -- all have been celebrated at the lake, in all seasons, and always with the Adirondack chairs around the fire pit.

And as my family has grown, our Adirondack chair collection has also grown. Besides my Westport chair and Sears Adirondack chair, there are now three more wooden Adirondack chairs and four new plastic Adirondack chairs in multiple colors. I watch all the activity, the celebrations with a slightly detached eye, remembering when I actively planned the events that now I just attend.

Rosie In Her Late Winter, Again

My 90th birthday party was a huge success with my children, grandchildren, my first great-grandchild, and friends all gathered to celebrate. How wonderful, how hopeful, how full of love! At the end of this wintry day, I see again my green chair in the tiny backyard. It reminds me of so many seasons of the year and of my life. Spring will soon come again, and those chairs will need some washing, sanding, and a new coat of paint…

About the Author

Kathleen Graham Kelly is a native of Albany, New York who grew up loving the Adirondack Park. Personally she is a wife, mother, grandmother, sister, aunt, and friend. Professionally she has been a teacher at every level of public education from kindergarten to university graduate level, with twenty years spent as a middle level reading teacher. Kathleen has also been an educational administrator; a grant manager, a staff developer, a teacher leader, and an employee of the state teachers' union and New York State Education Department. Her areas of expertise and interest include literacy, professional development for educators, adult development stages of growth, strategic planning for organizations, education for members of non-profit organization boards, and organizational learning. She holds a Bachelor of Arts degree in English Education and Master's degrees in Education and in Public Administration from the State University of New York at Albany, as well as a Doctoral degree in Organizational Leadership from Teachers' College, Columbia University, New York City.

Currently, Kathleen is a writer living in Schroon Lake, New York and Hilton Head Island, South Carolina. She is owner of Global Next Steps, a professional life-coaching enterprise. Kathleen is available to provide inspirational keynote addresses and to guide organizational retreats. She also provides individual and group coaching. For more information, go to GlobalNextSteps.com and globalnextsteps@facebook.com . To explore coaching or other services or to send a personal message, please send an email to coach@globalnextsteps.com

About the Photographer

Karen Rusinski Williamson developed a strong interest in conservation and the out-of-doors as a Girl Scout while growing up in Elma, New York (near Buffalo). She attended Syracuse University, where she majored in Photojournalism and minored in Environmental Studies.

After graduating, Karen worked for the U. S. Department of Agriculture's Soil Conservation Service (USDA SCS) as a photographer and communications specialist in New Hampshire and New York. Subsequently, she served in various communications positions with New York State, including the New York State Soil and Water Conservation Committee, the Department of Environmental Conservation and finally the Department of Labor. Throughout these years, Karen continued to operate a freelance photography business (Natural Images Photography) specializing in nature and landscape photography. Her work has appeared in many environmentally-related publications and art shows, and is currently carried in fine art and gift galleries in and near the Adirondacks.

Karen was introduced to the Adirondacks just after college, first on a climb of Blue Mountain with friends and then by a work assignment to write and illustrate a magazine article about how the SCS helped develop facilities for the 1980 Olympics. Her love for and connection to the Adirondacks has continued and deepened through years of day hikes, vacations, and camping trips in the Park with family and friends.

Karen lives in Guilderland and Saranac Inn, New York, with her husband, two Boston Terriers, and several Adirondack chairs. She enjoys canoeing, cross-country skiing, hiking, and spending time with friends and family, especially her two adult children and new son-in-law. You can see more of Karen's photography on her website at karenwilliamsonphoto.photoshelter.com

About the Adirondack Park

The Adirondack Park was created in 1892 by the State of New York amid concerns about degradation of the water and timber resources of the region. Today the Adirondack Park is the largest publicly-protected area in the contiguous United States; greater in size than Yellowstone, Everglades, Glacier, and Grand Canyon National Parks combined. The boundary of the park encompasses approximately 6 million acres, nearly half of which is state-owned and managed; it belongs to all the people of New York State. The remaining half of the park is private land, which includes settlements, farms, timberlands, businesses, resorts, homes, and camps.

The Adirondack Park is protected by Article XIV of the New York State Constitution to remain "forever wild" forest preserve, a law enacted by the NYS legislature in 1912.

The Adirondack Park's boundary is outlined with a blue line on state maps; hence, Adirondackers say they live within the "Blue Line." The Park contains 102 towns and villages with a year-round total population of 132,000, plus an additional 200,000 seasonal residents. Also included in the Park are upwards of 10,000 lakes, 30,000 miles of rivers and streams, and a wide variety of natural habitats, including wetlands and old-growth forests.

Source http://www.dec.ny.gov/lands/4960.html
Source https://www.apa.ny.gov/About_Park/index.html

About the Adirondack Chair

The Adirondack chair has a distinctive profile of a plank slanted back, slanted legs, and wide arms. It was originally designed as and still is considered primarily an outdoor chair; although the actual design and materials of construction have continued to evolve.

The prototype emerged in the early 1900s as an outdoor wooden chair designed by Thomas Lee and built by carpenter Harry Bunnell in Westport, New York, located just outside the edge of the Adirondack Park. Bunnell built Lee's design and obtained a patent for it in 1905. He manufactured the chairs for thirty years from a shop in Westport and painted them medium dark brown or green.

The lineage of the chair can be traced back to outdoor sanatorium treatment centers in the Adirondack Mountains. Here, tuberculosis patients sought a cure which included sitting outdoors in the clean mountain air for days, in all seasons. The so-called "Cure Chair" hints at the later design of the slanted back and legs of the Adirondack chair. The Morris chair, Cape Cod chair, the Canadian Muskoka chair and common deck chairs are also considered cousins of the classic Adirondack chair. Some furniture historians contend that the Adirondack chair shares design elements with some of the Arts and Crafts Movement furniture in vogue at the time of the chair's creation, as well as furniture created by Frank Lloyd Wright.

The Adirondack chair became popular as people began buying homes and moving from cities to suburbs where they needed chairs for their backyards. Adirondack chairs were relatively inexpensive to purchase, or could easily be made in home woodshops using minimal tools. Even today, towns throughout the Adirondack Park feature Adirondack chairs made by individual

woodworkers and small production shops. The annual Rustic Furniture Festival at the Adirondack Experience, The Museum on Blue Mountain Lake, showcases the wide variety of traditional and modern Adirondack chairs.

Adirondack chairs have traditionally been made from wooden planks of different woods available locally, but recently the design has been adapted and made in plastic in China and other places outside the United States. Modifications have been made to the original patented idea: different numbers of planks in the back and seat, a straight or rounded back, the addition of matching footstools, double-wide chairs, and swings. But the slanted shape of the design remains constant. You know one when you see one.

Not everyone loves sitting in an Adirondack chair. They slant back more than is comfortable for some people. Sometimes one's head is not well-supported. They are made from wood with no contouring so they are not easy on the spine for some. The arms slope toward the back so it is dangerous to rest your coffee cup or beer glass there. Most significantly they can be very difficult to get out of for certain persons. You don't want to be very pregnant and sit in one of these chairs. Often, Adirondack chair sitters need someone to lend a hand to pull them up from the chair.

Yet some beg to differ with the disadvantages listed! They find the plank flatness great on the back and argue that you can always get a pad if you feel the chair is too hard. Many put drinks on the arm and find that aspect one of the most convenient and appealing features of the chair! And some were even able to get out of my chairs when pregnant.

If a particular Adirondack chair doesn't agree with you, try another. The angles are all different, and the plastic ones are now contoured, too.

Sources Consulted

Bowie, Mark. *The Adirondacks: In Celebration of the Seasons.* 2009. 1st Edition, North Country Books.

Mack, Daniel. *The Adirondack Chair. A Celebration of a Summer Classic.* 2008. Stewart, Tabouri & Chang. China.

Wagner, John D. *Building Adirondack Furniture. The Art, The History, and the How-To.* 1995. Williamson Publishing. Charlotte, VT.

http://www.dec.ny.gov/lands/4960.html

Special Thanks To:

- Christine Perham, manuscript editor;

- Tony Kostecki, General Director, Seagle Colony, Schroon Lake, NY for a one-year loan of a green Westport-style Adirondack chair; and

- Bob Curry and family of Curry's Cottages in Blue Mountain Lake, NY. Their outstanding hospitality through the years is much appreciated, and their line of iconic Adirondack chairs on the lakeshore was the source of much creative inspiration for photographer Karen Williamson.

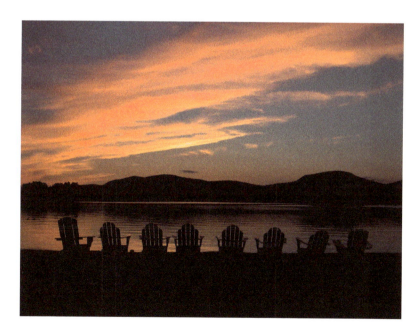

Follow

Web site www.achairforallseasons.com

In the future, look for and participate in preserving and expanding the image of the iconic Adirondack chair.

A Chair for All Seasons, Volume 2
Adirondack Chair Memories2

Volume 2 will be a collection of short memories (up to one thousand words) of family stories that include or are triggered by the memory of an Adirondack chair. Submissions may include photographs. Send your proposed submissions to Kathleen Graham Kelly at KathleenGK@gmail.com by December 31, 2019.

CPSIA information can be obtained
at www.ICGtesting.com
Printed in the USA
BVHW020427220119
538285BV00028B/1774/P